10 Unaccompanied Duets for F Horn or E♭ Horn

Gospel For Two

Table of Contents

⬤ Demo version

⬤ Play-along version (second part only)

Order Number: CMP 1227-07-400

James Curnow
GOSPEL FOR TWO
F Horn / E♭ Horn

ISBN: 978-90-431-2865-0

CD number: 19-092-3 CMP

Ten Unaccompanied Duets in a Gospel style
For any instruments

Greetings!

Music has no boundaries and should be performed and enjoyed by all who participate, either as a performer or as a listener. Emanating from African American spirituals and heavily influenced by the early New Orleans jazz musicians, Gospel music has been around for hundreds of years and has a sound, soul and joy all its own. Gospel songs add joy and happiness to our worship and other special events. It is universal in acceptance.

These easy duets are designed to allow the average to advanced players the opportunity to perform ten familiar Gospel songs in school, in church or any social occasion. No accompaniment is necessary. They may be played by any combination of woodwind, brass, string or mallet percussion instruments.

Below is an instrumentation guide that tells you the appropriate book to purchase for your instrument.

Most of all have fun and enjoy making music.

James Curnow
Composer/arranger

Instrumentation Guide

<u>C Instruments</u> (CMP 1224-07-400) Violin, Piccolo, Flute, Oboe, or any mallet percussion instrument.

<u>B♭ Instruments</u> (CMP 1226-07-400) Clarinet, Bass Clarinet, Cornet, Trumpet, Flugel Horn, Tenor Saxophone, Trombone T.C., Euphonium/Baritone T.C., Tuba T.C. (play second part only).

<u>E♭ Instruments</u> (CMP 1225-07-400) Alto Clarinet, Alto Saxophone, Baritone Saxophone (play second part only), Tenor (Alto) Horn, Tuba T.C. (play second part only).

<u>Horn F/E♭</u> (CMP 1227-07-400) F Horn, E♭ Horn, English Horn

<u>Bass Clef Instruments</u> (CMP 1228-07-400) Cello, Double Bass (play second part only), Bassoon, Trombone, Euphonium/Baritone, Tuba (play second part only).

SWING LOW, SWEET CHARIOT

F Horn

Arr. by **James Curnow** (ASCAP)

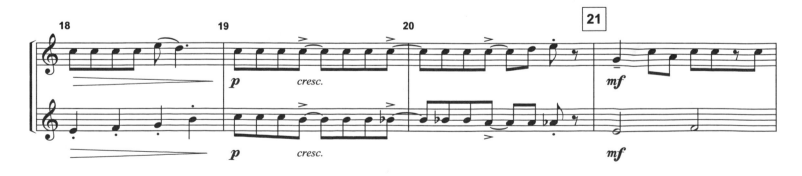

AMAZING GRACE

Arr. by **James Curnow** (ASCAP)

EVERY TIME I FEEL THE SPIRIT

Arr. by **James Curnow** (ASCAP)

HE'S GOT THE WHOLE WORLD IN HIS HANDS

Arr. by **James Curnow** (ASCAP)

FACE TO FACE

Arr. by **James Curnow** (ASCAP)

GO, TELL IT ON THE MOUNTAIN

Arr. by **James Curnow** (ASCAP)

I'M SO GLAD, JESUS LIFTED ME

Arr. by **James Curnow** (ASCAP)

NOBODY KNOWS THE TROUBLE I'VE SEEN

Arr. by **James Curnow** (ASCAP)

STEAL AWAY

Arr. by **James Curnow** (ASCAP)

SWEET BY AND BY

Arr. by **James Curnow** (ASCAP)

SWING LOW, SWEET CHARIOT

Arr. by **James Curnow** (ASCAP)

Eb Horn

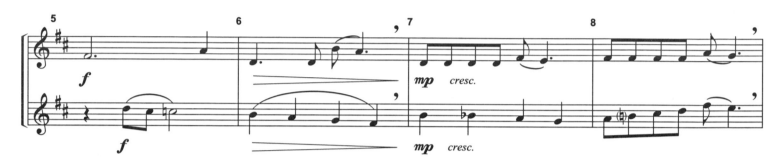

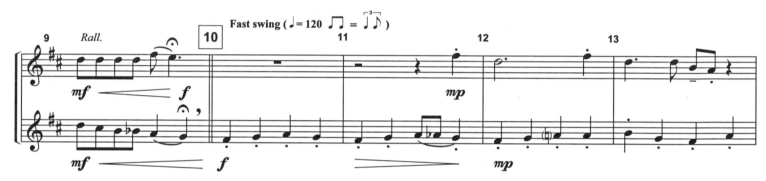

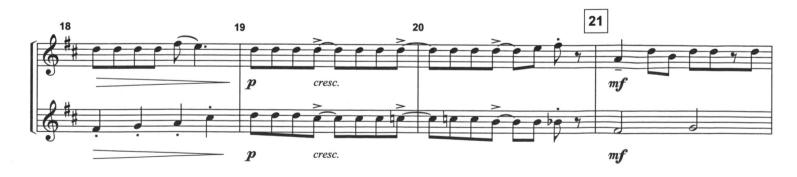

*Upper Octave is optional in all arrangements

AMAZING GRACE

Arr. by **James Curnow** (ASCAP)

EVERY TIME I FEEL THE SPIRIT

Arr. by **James Curnow** (ASCAP)

HE'S GOT THE WHOLE WORLD IN HIS HANDS

Arr. by **James Curnow** (ASCAP)

FACE TO FACE

Arr. by **James Curnow** (ASCAP)

GO, TELL IT ON THE MOUNTAIN

Arr. by **James Curnow** (ASCAP)

I'M SO GLAD, JESUS LIFTED ME

Arr. by **James Curnow** (ASCAP)

NOBODY KNOWS THE TROUBLE I'VE SEEN

Arr. by **James Curnow** (ASCAP)

STEAL AWAY

Arr. by **James Curnow** (ASCAP)

SWEET BY AND BY

Arr. by **James Curnow** (ASCAP)

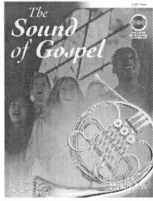

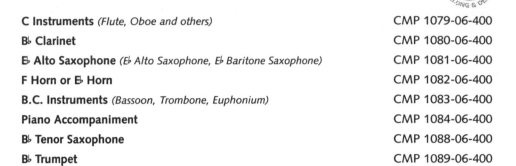

THE SOUND OF GOSPEL

C Instruments *(Flute, Oboe and others)*	CMP 1079-06-400
B♭ Clarinet	CMP 1080-06-400
E♭ Alto Saxophone *(E♭ Alto Saxophone, E♭ Baritone Saxophone)*	CMP 1081-06-400
F Horn or E♭ Horn	CMP 1082-06-400
B.C. Instruments *(Bassoon, Trombone, Euphonium)*	CMP 1083-06-400
Piano Accompaniment	CMP 1084-06-400
B♭ Tenor Saxophone	CMP 1088-06-400
B♭ Trumpet	CMP 1089-06-400

Arranged by Stephen Bulla

TWO FOR CHRISTMAS

C Instruments *(Flute, Oboe and others)*	CMP 0345-00-401
B♭ Instruments *(B♭ Clarinet, B♭ Trumpet, and others)*	CMP 0346-00-401
E♭ Instruments *(E♭ Alto Saxophone and others)*	CMP 0347-00-401
F Horn or E♭ Horn	CMP 0348-00-401
B.C. Instruments *(Bassoon, Trombone, Euphonium and others)*	CMP 0349-00-401

James Curnow

TWO FOR EASTER

C Instruments *(Flute, Oboe and others)*	CMP 1135-06-401
B♭ Instruments *(B♭ Clarinet, Bb Trumpet and others)*	CMP 1136-06-401
E♭ Instruments *(E♭ Alto Saxophone and others)*	CMP 1137-06-401
F Horn or E♭ Horn	CMP 1138-06-401
B.C. Instruments *(Trombone, Euphonium and others)*	CMP 1139-06-401

James Curnow